Grandmother's Book

BY

MARCIA O. LEVIN

HUGH LAUTER LEVIN ASSOCIATES, INC.

ILLUSTRATIONS

James Jabusa Shannon
JUNGLE TALES
1895
oil on canvas
34¾ × 44¾"
The Metropolitan Museum of Art, New York
Arthur Hoppock Hearn Fund, 1913

Anonymous
BIRTH AND BAPTISMAL CERTIFICATE OF ANNE ANDRES
c. 1783
pen and iron gall ink with watercolor on laid paper
13¼ × 16"
National Gallery of Art, Washington, D.C.
Gift of Edgar William and Bernice Chrysler Garbisch

Joseph H. Davis
JOHN AND ABIGAIL MONTGOMERY
1836
pen and watercolor
8⅞ × 14"
National Gallery of Art, Washington, D.C.
Gift of Edgar William and Bernice Chrysler Garbisch

Edouard Vuillard
THEODORE DURET
1912
cardboard mounted on wood
37½ × 29½"
National Gallery of Art, Washington, D.C.
Chester Dale Collection

Carl Schaefer
ONTARIO FARM HOUSE
1934
oil on canvas
42 × 49⅛"
National Gallery of Canada, Ottawa
Gift of Floyd S. Chalmers, Toronto, 1969
Reproduced by permission of the artist

Winslow Homer
HOMEWORK
1874
watercolor
8 × 5"
Canajoharie Library and Art Gallery, New York

Frank W. Benson
PORTRAIT OF MY DAUGHTERS
1907
oil on canvas
26⅛ × 36⅛"
Worcester Art Museum, Massachusetts

Norman Rockwell
STORYTELLER
1945
oil on canvas
46 × 42"
The Norman Rockwell Museum at Stockbridge, Massachusetts
Printed by permission of the Estate of Norman Rockwell
Copyright © 1945, Estate of Norman Rockwell

Mary Cassatt
ALEXANDER CASSATT AND HIS SON ROBERT
1884–85
oil on canvas
39 × 32"
Philadelphia Museum of Art
W. P. Wilstach Collection

Grandma Moses
A COUNTRY WEDDING
1951
oil on Masonite
17 × 22"
Copyright © 1973, Grandma Moses Properties Co., New York

Norman Rockwell
FREEDOM FROM FEAR
1943
oil on canvas
45¾ × 35½"
The Norman Rockwell Museum at Stockbridge, Massachusetts
Printed by permission of the Estate of Norman Rockwell
Copyright © 1943, Estate of Norman Rockwell

Norman Rockwell
FAMILY TREE
1959
oil on canvas
46 × 42"
The Norman Rockwell Museum at Stockbridge, Massachusetts
Printed by permission of the Estate of Norman Rockwell
Copyright © 1959, Estate of Norman Rockwell

Grandma Moses
ROCKABYE
1957
oil on Masonite
11⅞ × 16"
Private collection
Copyright © 1973, Grandma Moses Properties Co., New York

Wayne Thiebaud
BUFFET
1972–75
oil on canvas
48 × 60"
Private collection
Courtesy Allan Stone Gallery, New York

Norman Rockwell
FREEDOM FROM WANT
1943
oil on canvas
45¾ × 35½"
Printed by permission of the Estate of Norman Rockwell
Copyright © 1943, Estate of Norman Rockwell

Picture research: Ann Levy

Calligraphy: Gunta Alexander

Dedication

This is a book of memories
lovingly recorded by

_____

and given to

_____

JUNGLE TALES—James Jabusa Shannon

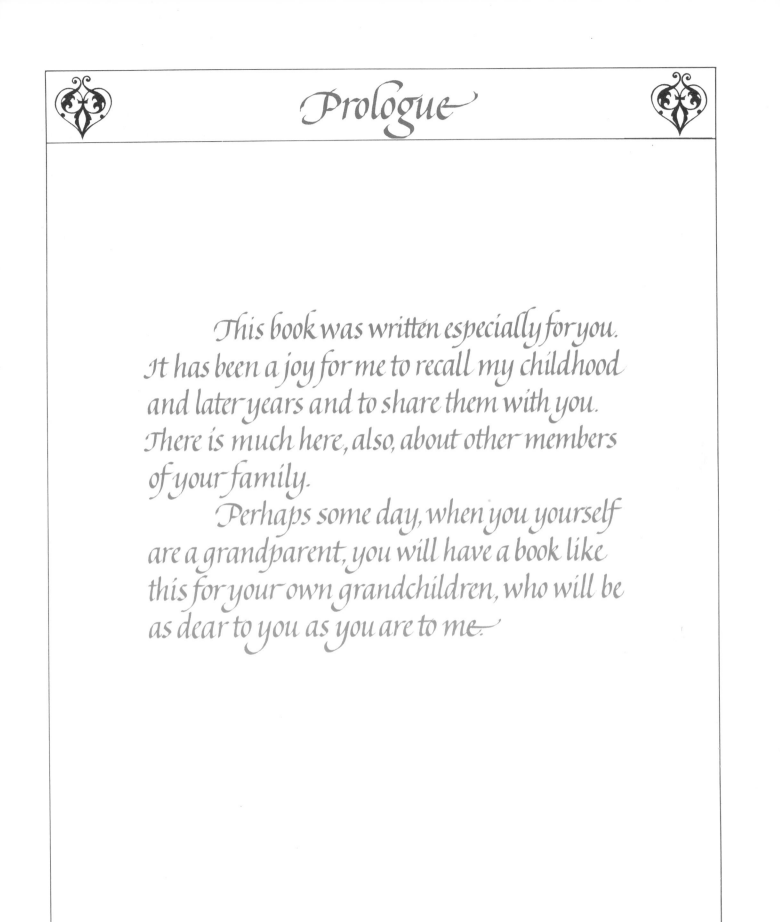

Prologue

This book was written especially for you. It has been a joy for me to recall my childhood and later years and to share them with you. There is much here, also, about other members of your family.

Perhaps some day, when you yourself are a grandparent, you will have a book like this for your own grandchildren, who will be as dear to you as you are to me.

My Picture

Here is what I looked like
when I filled out this book.

Paste
a recent
picture
of yourself
here.

Date_____

The name you always call me is

_____

My Picture

'Backward, turn backward, O Time, in your flight,
Make me a child again just for tonight.'

~ Elizabeth Allen (1832-1911)

Paste
a childhood
picture
of yourself
here.

This is the earliest picture of me.
I was _____ years old.

My Birth

My full name is _____

I was named that because _____

_____

_____

The date of my birth was _____

The place of my birth was _____

Other things you might like to know about my birth.

_____

_____

_____

_____

_____

_____

_____

_____

_____

_____

BIRTH AND BAPTISMAL CERTIFICATE OF ANNE ANDRES—Anonymous

My Mother's Side

_____

My Mother
Your Great-grandmother

_____
My Mother's Mother
(My grandmother was your
great-great-grandmother.)

_____
My Mother's Father
(My grandfather was your
great-great-grandfather.)

_____
My Mother's Grandmother
(My great-grandmother
was your great-great-great-
grandmother.)

_____
My Mother's Grandmother
(My great-grandmother
was your great-great-great-
grandmother.)

_____
My Mother's Grandfather
(My great-grandfather
was your great-great-great-
grandfather.)

_____
My Mother's Grandfather
(My great-grandfather
was your great-great-great-
grandfather.)

My Father's Side

My Father
Your Great-grandfather

My Father's Mother
(My grandmother was your great-great-grandmother.)

My Father's Father
(My grandfather was your great-great-grandfather.)

My Father's Grandmother
(My great-grandmother was your great-great-great-grandmother.)

My Father's Grandmother
(My great-grandmother was your great-great-great-grandmother.)

My Father's Grandfather
(My great-grandfather was your great-great-great-grandfather.)

My Father's Grandfather
(My great-grandfather was your great-great-great-grandfather.)

It is indeed desirable to be well descended,
but glory belongs to our ancestors. —Plutarch (46-120 A.D.)

My mother's mother's birth place was _____
   Her birth date was _____
My mother's father's birth place was _____
   His birth date was _____
Where they lived when I knew them _____
What I remember best about them is _____
_____
_____

My father's mother's birth place was _____
   Her birth date was _____
My father's father's birth place was _____
   His birth date was _____
Where they lived when I knew them _____
What I remember best about them is _____
_____
_____

JOHN AND ABIGAIL MONTGOMERY—*Joseph H. Davis*

My Parents

Who ran to help me when I fell,
And would some pretty story tell,
Or kiss the place to make it well?
My mother. —Ann Taylor (1782-1866)

My mother's full name was _____

    Her birth place _____

    Her birth date _____

    Her education and occupation were _____

_____

My father's full name was _____

    His birth place _____

    His birth date _____

    His education and occupation were _____

_____

Their marriage took place in _____

    on _____

Where they lived _____

_____

My Mother

Here are some things I would like you to know
about my mother.

_____

_____

_____

_____

_____

_____

_____

_____

_____

_____

_____

_____

_____

_____

My Father

One father is more than a hundred schoolmasters.

—George Herbert (1593-1633)

Here are some things I would like you to know about my father.

_____

_____

_____

_____

_____

_____

_____

_____

_____

_____

_____

_____

THEODORE DURET—Edouard Vuillard

These are my sisters, brothers and other
relatives who have been important to me.

Name _____

Relationship to me _____

Name _____

Relationship to me _____

Name _____

Relationship to me _____

Name _____

Relationship to me _____

Other Family Members

Name _____

Relationship to me _____

Name _____

Relationship to me _____

Name _____

Relationship to me _____

Name _____

Relationship to me _____

Name _____

Relationship to me _____

My Home

I remember, I remember
The house where I was born,
The little window where the sun
Came peeping in at morn.
—Thomas Hood (1799-1845)

The home where I lived as a child was in _____

_____

I remember this about my home. _____

_____

_____

_____

_____

_____

_____

ONTARIO FARM HOUSE—Carl Schaefer

I have more memories than if I were a thousand years old.

—Baudelaire (1821-1867)

Can you remember things that happened when you were very, very small? I was once that small too, and here are a few things I remember from those days.

_____

_____

_____

_____

_____

_____

_____

_____

_____

_____

_____

Even a child is renown by his doings, whether
his work be pure, and whether it be right.

—*Proverbs 20:11*

Here are a few of the funny, or clever, or unusual incidents in my early life that my parents enjoyed telling about.

_____

_____

_____

_____

_____

_____

_____

_____

_____

23

My School Days

School days, school days,
Dear old Golden Rule days!

These are the schools I attended.

Name _____

Its location was _____

My most vivid memory is _____

_____

Name _____

Its location was _____

My most vivid memory is _____

_____

Name _____

Its location was _____

My most vivid memory is _____

_____

HOMEWORK—Winslow Homer

My School Days

The days that make us happy make us wise.
—John Masefield (1878-1967)

The subject I liked most was _____
because _____
The subject I liked least was _____
because _____
My after-school activities were _____

_____

_____

My other interests included _____

_____

_____

I was proudest when _____

_____

_____

My Friends

I have had playmates, I have had companions,
In my days of childhood, in my joyful school days.

— Charles Lamb (1775-1834)

My friends were _____

_____

_____

Our favorite meeting place was _____

_____

Our pastimes included _____

_____

_____

_____

The most fun we had was when _____

_____

_____

My very best friend was _____
because _____

Nothing endures but change —Heraclitus (540-480 B.C.)

When I was young the style of dress for girls was _____

_____

_____

The style of dress for boys was _____

_____

The popular hairstyles were _____

_____

Fashions and fads of the time included _____

_____

_____

_____

_____

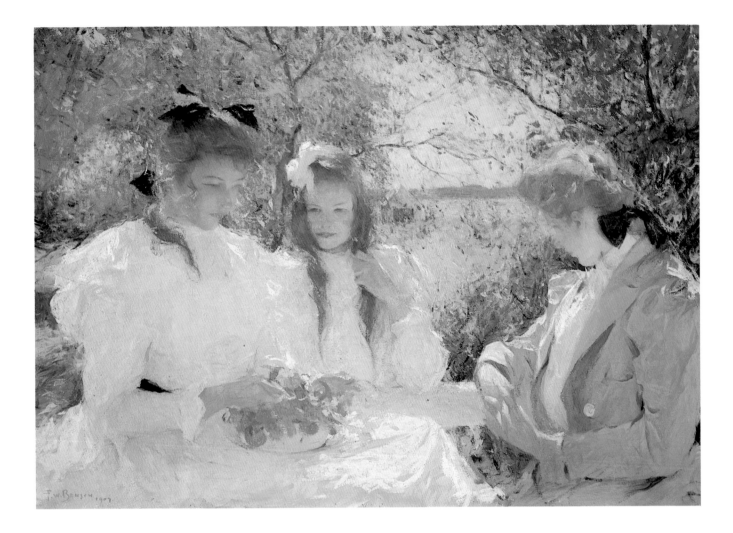

PORTRAIT OF MY DAUGHTERS—Frank W. Benson

The popular music was _____

_____

_____

Popular singers I liked most included _____

_____

_____

My favorite dances were _____

_____

_____

The inventions that appeared when I was young
 included _____

_____

_____

_____

The most exciting discoveries made in those days were ___

_____

_____

_____

My Favorites Then

When the dog bites,
When the bee stings,
When I'm feeling sad,
I simply remember my favorite things,
And then I don't feel so bad.

— Oscar Hammerstein (1895-1960)

Family member _____

Teacher _____

Game _____

Hobby _____

Book _____

Entertainment _____

Holiday _____

Vacation _____

_____

Foods _____

_____

Pets _____

_____

Certain events that occur while we are growing up remain memorable. Whether we were six years old or sixteen at the time, we can recall not only when they happened, but what we were doing when we heard the news. Here are a few of the events that left a lasting impression on me.

_____

_____

_____

_____

_____

_____

_____

_____

_____

_____

_____

_____

_____

STORYTELLER—Norman Rockwell

Your Grandfather

Oh, talk not to me of a name great in story;
The days of our youth are the days of our glory.

—Lord Byron (1788–1824)

Your grandfather's full name was _____

_____

The way we met was _____

_____

_____

_____

Our ages when we met were _____

_____

My first impression of him was _____

_____

_____

Our first real date was _____

_____

_____

Your grandfather was born in _____

_____

His birth date was _____

The place where he grew up was _____

_____

His parents were _____

_____

_____

_____

Other things about his family were _____

_____

_____

_____

Other things about his background and education were

_____

_____

_____

_____

As we began to know each other better, I learned these things about the man I was going to marry.

His work was _____

_____

His ambition was _____

The books he liked were _____

_____

His favorite sport was _____

_____

The foods he enjoyed were _____

_____

The entertainment he preferred was _____

_____

What I liked most about him was _____

_____

_____

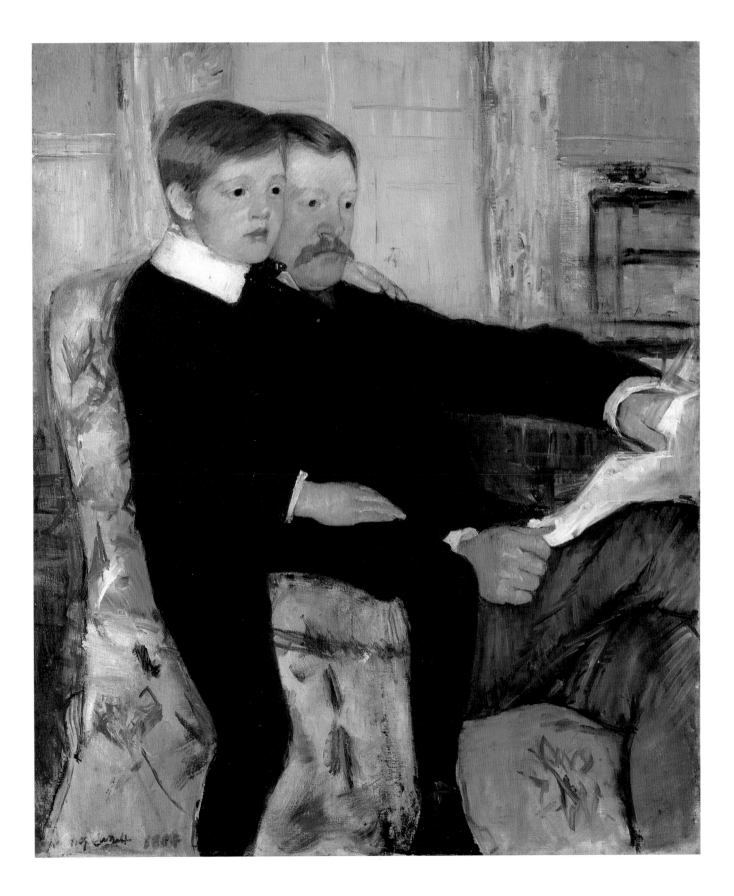

ALEXANDER CASSATT AND HIS SON ROBERT—*Mary Cassatt*

Our Wedding

My true love hath my heart, and I have his,
By just exchange one for the other given.
— Sir Philip Sidney (1554-1586)

We decided to get married after knowing each other _____

_____

The way we told our families and friends was _____

_____

_____

The way we planned our wedding was _____

_____

_____

The date of our wedding was _____
The ceremony took place at _____

_____

We invited relatives and friends, including _____

_____

_____

_____

Our Wedding

Wedding gifts I remember were _____

_____

_____

_____

I wore _____

_____

_____

The groom wore _____

_____

Our attendants were _____

_____

_____

The wedding meal was _____

_____

_____

My feeling that day was _____

_____

_____

Our Marriage

A woman's whole life is a history of the affections.
—Washington Irving (1783-1859)

On our honeymoon we went to _____

_____

Our first home was _____

_____

What I remember about our home is _____

_____

The way I spent my days was _____

_____

The way your grandfather spent his days was _____

_____

Our first anniversary was _____

_____

Our early challenges included _____

_____

_____

A COUNTRY WEDDING—Grandma Moses

Your Parent

Rock-a-bye baby, on the tree top.
When the wind blows, the cradle will rock.
—Charles Blake (1846-1903)

Some memories of my child, who grew up
to be your parent, include
  Date of birth _____
  Place of birth _____
  We chose the name _____
  The reason for the name was _____
  _____
  _____

First reactions to the baby included
  What I said _____
  _____
  _____

  What other people said _____
  _____
  _____

Time is but the stream I go a-fishing in.
—Henry David Thoreau (1817-1862)

It seems only yesterday that your parent was a little child, learning about the world. I still recall with fondness some of the things that happened then.

_____

_____

_____

_____

_____

_____

_____

_____

_____

Your Parent

How beautiful is youth! How bright it gleams,
With its illusions, aspiration, dreams!
Book of beginnings, story without end,
Each maid a heroine, and each man a friend.

—Salutamus

Here are some of the things you might like to know about your parent's growing-up years.

Schools attended _____

_____

_____

Special abilities _____

_____

_____

Special interests _____

_____

_____

Hobbies _____

_____

_____

FREEDOM FROM FEAR—Norman Rockwell

The Way It Was

The more things change, the more they remain the same.
–French Proverb

When your parent was a teenager, this is what was happening:

The style of dress for girls was _____

_____

The style of dress for boys was _____

_____

Fashions and fads of that time were _____

_____

The music that was popular was _____

_____

Popular dances were _____

_____

The inventions of the day included _____

_____

The most exciting discoveries were _____

_____

There's nothing half so sweet in life
As love's young dream. —Thomas Moore (1779-1852)

The place they met was _____

_____

Their ages were _____

_____

Our first meeting was _____

_____

_____

The place they were married was _____

_____

The date of the ceremony was _____
My memories of that day include _____

_____

_____

_____

_____

You Are Born

Around the child tend all the three
Sweet Graces: Faith, Hope, Charity.
—Walter Savage Landor (1775-1864)

Your birthday was _____

You were born in _____

You weighed _____

You were named by _____

That name was chosen because _____

_____

Other things I remember about your birth include _____

_____

_____

_____

_____

_____

_____

FAMILY TREE—Norman Rockwell

Oft in the stilly night,
Ere Slumber's chain has bound me,
Fond Memory brings the light
Of other days around me. —Thomas Moore (1779-1852)

How delighted I was to hear that you had arrived! I couldn't wait to see you.

The place where I heard was _____

_____

What I was doing was _____

_____

I first saw you when _____

_____

The first time I took care of you was _____

_____

I remember you as the kind of baby who _____

_____

_____

Give a little love to a child, and you get a great deal back.
~John Ruskin (1819-1900)

The songs I sang to you were _____

_____

_____

Your favorite story was _____

The games we played included _____

_____

_____

Your favorite toys were _____

_____

Your favorite gifts from me were _____

_____

_____

Your Visits to Me

The length of your stay was usually _____

You usually came with _____

_____

Our favorite pastimes were _____

_____

_____

_____

I think you liked my home because _____

_____

_____

I remember the time when you _____

_____

_____

_____

ROCKABYE—Grandma Moses

Grandmother Remembers You

I remember a trip we took together.

The place we went was _____

_____

The date of the trip was _____
The way we traveled was _____

_____

With us was _____

_____

My special memory of that trip is _____

_____

_____

_____

Other places we went together were _____

_____

_____

Your favorite outing was _____

_____

You Remember Grandmother

I have saved a page so that you can help me finish our book, for it should be yours as well as mine.

Your earliest memory of me is _____

_____

_____

_____

Other things you remember include _____

_____

_____

_____

_____

_____

_____

_____

_____

My Favorites Now

Times change, and we change with them.

—Edmund Spenser (1552-1599)

Game _____

Hobby _____

_____

Book _____

_____

Movie _____

_____

Television program _____

Holiday _____

_____

Vacation _____

_____

Friend _____

Foods _____

_____

BUFFET—Wayne Thiebaud

My Ideas and Ideals

Oh that my words were now written !
Oh that they were printed in a book ! — Job 19:23

Certain things have always been most important to me. I would like to share some of them with you, both because I'd like you to understand the kind of person I have been and because some day you too may feel that they are important.

_____

_____

_____

_____

_____

_____

_____

_____

_____

Family Sayings

Give your ears to hear the sayings,
Give your heart to understand them.
—Amenemope (11th Century B.C.)

Some members of our family were known for their pet phrases, which could be funny or clever or silly or wise. Here are a few of them and who said them.

_____

_____

_____

_____

_____

_____

_____

_____

Every tradition grows more venerable.... The reverence due to it increases from generation to generation.

—Friedrich Nietzsche (1844-1900)

Each family does certain things in its own special manner. From the way we celebrate birthdays and holidays to the kinds of food we eat, traditions are an important means of tying us together. Here are some traditions that I hope you will continue.

_____

_____

_____

_____

_____

_____

_____

_____

FREEDOM FROM WANT—Norman Rockwell

Kissing don't last: cookery do!
— George Meredith (1828-1909)

Here are the recipes for a few of the dishes that were always requested when the family came to visit me.

_____

_____

_____

_____

_____

_____

_____

_____

_____

_____

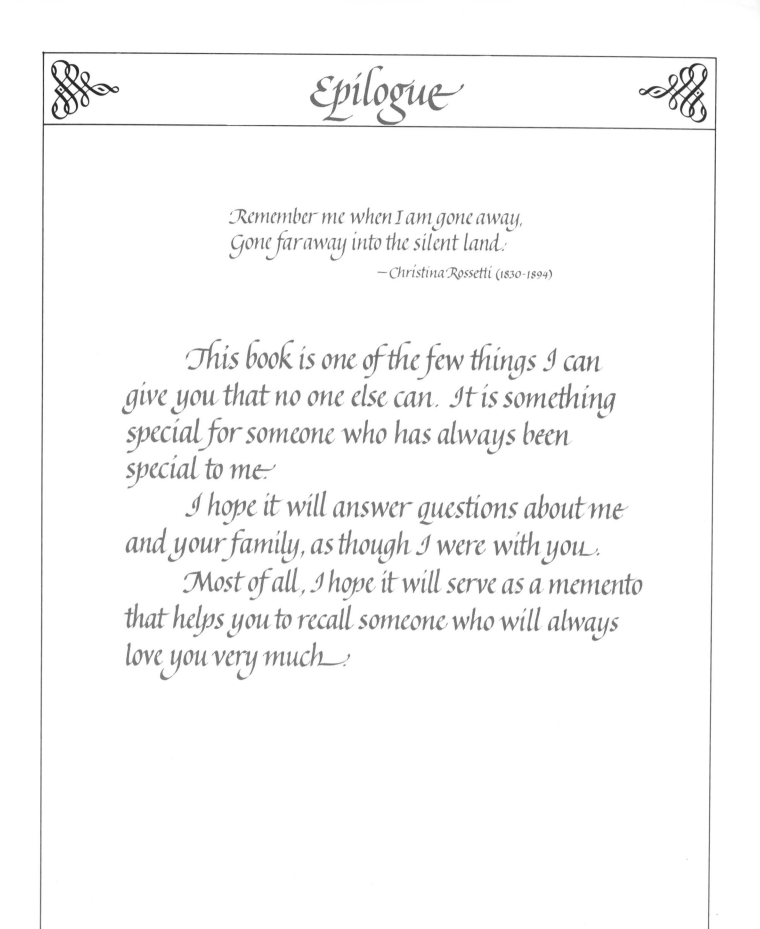

Epilogue

Remember me when I am gone away,
Gone far away into the silent land.

— Christina Rossetti (1830-1894)

      This book is one of the few things I can give you that no one else can. It is something special for someone who has always been special to me.

      I hope it will answer questions about me and your family, as though I were with you.

      Most of all, I hope it will serve as a memento that helps you to recall someone who will always love you very much.